Dear Readers,

We're so excited you're applying to college! Our founder is a graduate of Stanford University, an essay expert, and has helped hundreds of students gain admission to Ivy League and competitive schools. We hope to impart her insight to you in this essay workbook.

Email us for sneak-peeks and giveaways. Also check out our YouTube channel Fill In The Essay for helpful videos.

Happy writing!

*Fill In The Essay*

**@FillinTheEssay on IG, Twitter, YouTube**

*Fillintheessay.com*

*fillintheessay@gmail.com*

# Table of Contents

# PROMPT

**Discuss an accomplishment, event, or realization that sparked a period of personal growth and a new understanding of yourself or others.**

## BREAKING DOWN THE PROMPT

Over the next few pages, we'll help you understand this prompt inside and out. This prompt has several important elements to consider.

You undoubtedly have had an experience that helped you grow as a person before. About 20-25% of students have chosen this prompt historically because it's so universal. This prompt is also extremely popular because who doesn't like sharing some of the great things they've done before?

The key here is to be careful in choosing the proper accomplishment, event, or realization. There are a few cliché topics and common mistakes that we'll mention later in this workbook. For now though, let's break down this prompt thoroughly because this prompt has a lot of important parts to it. We'll tell you what you want to show admissions officers and how to do this effectively.

## "Discuss..."

To Discuss means to have a conversation, or to exchange ideas and opinions. For the purpose of the Common App it means the same as "reflect," "consider," or "contemplate." This means much more than to simply "write about" something or "describe" something. Discussion and Reflection require you to examine your inward motivations, answer *why* something matters to you, and how you have learned from an experience. It requires a level of self-awareness and critical thinking. The best essays are meaningful without being cliché, introspective, and show that you have learned or changed from an experience.

Here's an example of non-discursive vs discursive writing:

Non-discursive writing:

> *Every male in my family, from my great-great-grandfather to my father, has proudly served in the United States military. My family always went over-the-top for Fourth of July celebrations and Memorial Day. My grandfather can name over 100 historical generals and the battles they*

fought. My brother was recently deployed for a second tour of Afghanistan. They feel a call of duty beyond serving their country – military service runs as deep in my family as blood. I was convinced I would answer the call one I turned eighteen. All of this changed during my freshman year in high school, when I talked with a young military veteran at a recruitment session.

I expected to hear stories of bravery and valor, or kinship and brotherhood. But he was honest with his opinions. He said that many days he woke up and knew there was a hard day of work ahead. He divulged how he was a proud of his work but may have chosen a different career if he could do it over again. For the first time, my goals started to waver. Over the next several months I began questioning my motivations, seeking advice from teachers and mentors. I realized that I wanted to continue the family tradition of serving the *country, but that there were many ways to do so. I owed myself – and my country – more certainty before making such a decision.*

The above paragraph isn't horrible. It talks about a male student who always assumed he would join the military due to his family ties. It gives specific and descriptive examples showing the extent to which he felt he was going to enter the military. There is also a clear realization after the student talks to the young military recruiter.

But this paragraph does not provide good discourse for a couple of reasons. First, the change in his belief happened too quickly and too easily. A single event prompted the change, but we don't know *how* the recruiter changed his mind or *why* it caused him to think differently. If it only took one conversation to change his mind, then perhaps his reasons for choosing the military were poor. Second, the outcome of this experience is too one-dimensional: he simply changed his mind and doesn't explain how he explored various options.

Now, compare this paragraph with the paragraph below, which is much more reflective and meaningful.

Discursive writing:

*Every male in my family, from my great-great-grandfather to my father, has proudly served in the United States military. My family always went over-the-top for Fourth of July celebrations and Memorial Day. My grandfather can name over 100 historical generals and the battles they fought. My brother was recently deployed for a second tour of Afghanistan. They feel a call of duty beyond serving their country – military service runs as deep in my family as blood. I was convinced I would answer the call one I turned eighteen. All of this changed during my freshman year in high school, when I talked with a young military veteran at a recruitment session. I expected to hear stories of bravery and valor, or kinship and brotherhood.*

*But he was honest with his opinions. He said that many days he woke up and knew there was a hard day of work ahead. He divulged how he was a proud of his work but may have chosen a different career if he could do it over again. For the first time, my goals started to waver. The surprise of hearing about the nitty gritty of military service made me question if I had an idealized view of what it meant to serve.*

*Why should I join the military? Was it a true passion or a sense of obligation? Over the next several months I began questioning my motivations, seeking advice from teachers and mentors. I also turned to my father and grandfather for their reasons of joining the military. Surprisingly, my grandfather said he would not have volunteered had he not been drafted. My father also revealed that joining the Air Force was the only way he would have been able to afford a college education. I realized that I wanted to continue the family tradition of serving the country, but that there were many ways to do so.*

*I owed myself – and my country – more certainty before making such a decision. Now, I am optimistic about pursuing a college education. I know there are many ways I can contribute beyond military service. One day, I hope to become an engineer and contribute to better national infrastructure and transportation systems.*

Note that this paragraph is much more reflective. It looks inward to analyze the reasons . Although a single event (the conversation with the recruiter) sparked a change in the student, he also explored the other reasons for realizing the military may not be for him. For example, the surprising admissions from his father and grandfather about why they joined the military also influenced him. The student also faced his flaws by admitting he had idealized what military service was like. Overall, the student self-analyzes his limited point of view. We see internal conflict when he realizes his planned career path was not well-thought out, and we also see some resolution when he talks about other ways to serve his country. The writer is clearly mature and has put a lot of thought into this experience.

## "Accomplishment", "Event", or "Realization"

Since this prompt uses the word "or," you need only choose ONE of these things (either an accomplishment OR and event OR a realization) to write about. Don't make the common mistake of writing about multiple experiences that have influenced your life. This Common App prompt is

asking for you to write about one experience in detail, not the accumulation of multiple experiences. For example, you can write about the time you organized a protest march against homelessness. You shouldn't try to cover in detail about the first time you met a homeless person *and* your volunteering at the homeless shelter *and* organizing the protest march. You can mention related topics, but you should have a clear focus on one experience as this prompt asks. Don't spread yourself too thin.
Let's also talk about "Realization."

Accomplishments and Events are pretty easy to think of because they are concrete things that happened (becoming an Eagle Scout, being elected to student council, completing a Confirmation, etc.). A "realization" is a bit more abstract. In the context of this prompt, Realization is defined as a new awareness of something. There is often an element of surprise in realizations. Ultimately, you should show a definitive shift in your perspective as you be once more aware of the world around you. Some common coming-of-age realizations include:

- Experiencing newfound and increasing responsibilities of adulthood
- Challenging the authority of your parents/guardians and/or moving out of the house
- Reflecting on the role a mentor has had in your life
- Learning about societal inequities (homelessness, poverty, racism, sexism, prejudices, etc.)
- Exploring and accepting elements of personal identity (career goals, character traits, sexual orientation, etc.)
- Questioning previously held beliefs regarding religion, politics, cultural traditions, etc.
- Being forced to grow up too quickly due to hardships at home

- Looking back on how challenges and hard times have worked out for the best
- Trying out new activities and discovering new passions

Many of the aforementioned topics can be cliché if not written well. Make sure to read our Common Mistakes section for pitfalls to avoid. All of these topics listed can become stellar essays, but only if done correctly.

One thing you might also notice is that your essay topic doesn't have to be about something extravagant, shock-worthy, or of gargantuan magnitudes. In fact, oftentimes the best essays have simple topics. For example, one student chose to write about weekly hikes with her mother. As they spent more time together, they had deeper discussions about what thrilled, scared, or frustrated them in the world. The student began to see her mother as more than a parent who drove her to soccer practice and cooked dinner; she was also a concerned citizen and a freethinker. This realization was how the student knew she was transforming from a teenager to a young adult.

The most important part of choosing a topic that is meaningful to you, worthy of deep reflection, and the catalyst for personal change. You also want to choose a topic that's specific and unique to you. Many, if not all, students will have examples from the list above. We don't want your essay to sound too similar to other students' essays. We want your essay to stand out in the sea of applications that schools get each year.

Don't worry, we have tips and a step-by-step guide to choosing a topic in future sections of this workbook guide.

## "Period of Personal Growth"

Period implies a length of time. In other words, the personal growth cannot be instantaneous. Many students will think their essay has to have a sudden "AHA!" or "It was then that I realized..." moment. This simply isn't the case. In fact, writing that is over-the-top or exaggerated can often work against you. Don't try to impress the reader with a crazy story or sudden change in events. Instead, impress them with your maturity, writing quality, and sense of authenticity. Many deeply held beliefs take time to change, and it is quite valuable for admissions committees to see the *process* of your personal growth. Processes happen over time, not instantly. Therefore, you should give multiple specific examples of efforts you took to learn about yourself over a period of at least months (if not years).

What exactly is personal growth? It can be described as a change in your thoughts or actions that are better or more productive in some way – for you, for others, or for your greater community. I think it's best shown through plentiful examples:

- Educating yourself about current events to become a more informed citizen
- Altruistic actions like volunteering, lending a helping hand, and generally trying to be a better person
- Expanding your creative limits through art, music, writing, etc.
- Stepping outside of your comfort zone in some way in order to gain new skills
- Prioritizing healthful behaviors over irresponsible decisions
- Continually evaluating how your personal and career goals are changing
- Managing your time better if you're a procrastinator

- Learning to control your emotions in challenging situations
- Accepting increasing responsibility in order to help yourself or others
- Keeping an open mind

Importantly, note that personal growth requires intrinsic motivation, the desire for self-improvement, and deliberate effort.

Some universities are known for valuing certain types of personal growth. For example, Stanford University looks for students with "intellectual vitality" – your "commitment, dedication and genuine interest in expanding your intellectual horizons" and "the initiative with which you seek out opportunities and expand your perspective." Sounds like personal growth of the mind, right? Yale University similarly looks for a "desire and ability to stretch one's limits." In previous supplemental applications, Harvard University has also asked about "an intellectual experience," "unusual circumstances in your life," and "travel or living experiences in other countries" related to personal growth. Personal growth is key to future success (defined broadly) as you reach the milestone of pursuing a college education.

## "New Understanding"

Good news! If you've shown personal growth in your essay, then you've likely also addressed a "new understanding."

A simple way to show a "new" understanding is to show a clear "before" and "after" of yourself before the accomplishment, event, or realization. You should establish what the circumstances were *before* the catalytic event, the process as you experienced the event, and lastly follow up with *after* you had time to reflect on how you had changed.

In the "before" section, set the stage and give specific examples of everyday life and what you were like. For example, describe what your beliefs or goals were, *how ingrained* these beliefs were, and *the manifestations and consequences* of these beliefs.

Next, talk about the accomplishment, event, or realization that occurred. Tell the reader who you went to for advice during this time of change. Reveal the doubts you had as you question various aspects of your understanding. Show a high level of self-awareness about how you might have been incorrect or ignorant in the past. Remember our tips above about showing a process over a period of time.

Lastly, the "after" section should clearly contrast the "before" section. How did you change? By showing this change, you will portray yourself as someone who has great potential over the next few years as you adjust to the pressures and freedoms of college life. Your understanding of yourself, others, and ideas will continue to change in the future. Admissions committees also want to see if you are openminded or not. When you join a college campus you will be living and studying among students who have vastly different cultures, backgrounds, and opinions than you. The best students see this diversity as an opportunity to learn more about the world and seek connection with others. You can show open-mindedness in this essay by acknowledging how you have held flawed or incomplete views in the past, making an effort to understand different options, and how much you have left to learn.

## "Yourself or Others"

Most students will choose to write about periods of growth in "yourself" rather than "others." After all, communicating your thoughts is much easier when *you're* the one experiencing it and thinking about it. If you choose instead to talk about how you saw someone else go through a period of personal growth, make sure you explain your relationship to that person thoroughly.

# CHOOSING A TOPIC

Take enough time to choose a good topic for this prompt. Putting more thought into this now will save you a lot of time in the future.

Get Ready, because we're about to make writing your Common App first draft the easiest thing ever!

- First, we'll tell you which topics to AVOID.

- Second, we'll warn you about common essay MISTAKES.

- Third, we'll guide you through topic BRAINSTORMING.

- Lastly, we'll go step-by-step and line-by-line until you've written a COMPLETE FIRST DRAFT!

# TOPICS TO AVOID:

We've read hundreds of essays and these topics are cliché, overused, and/or full of pitfalls!

Try to avoid choosing one of these topics so that your essay has the best chance of standing out:

- Stories from early childhood
    - If you were a young child, chances are you don't remember the event as well as one that happened more recently. There are probably more meaningful events you can write about that occurred in high school rather than ones when you were 8 years old.
- Gory events
    - Seeing severe injuries or health scares can definitely make people change. Just make sure you don't aim for shock-value with over-the-top descriptions.

- Red Flag events
  - Everyone makes mistakes, but incidents involving Drugs/Alcohol/Breaking the law/Lacking professionalism at school or work may lead to an immediate rejection of your application.
- Romantic encounters
  - Admissions officers don't want to hear about your high school relationship(s). Enough said.
- Travel or Trips, especially to faraway locations
  - This is a common topic for many students who go on mission trips, volunteering trips, or school exchange programs. Unfortunately, essays on these topics are rarely executed well because they often oversimplify cultural differences.

- Failing to make the team (sports or otherwise), and trying again next year
  - Stories about learning the value of hard work and dedication are a dime a dozen. It would be *very* hard to make an essay on this topic memorable.
- Failing to win the championship or big game
  - See the explanation above, as the same reasons apply.
- Failing a test
  - Again, see the explanation above.

A side note about this list is that almost every topic has already been covered in a Common App essay. Admissions officers read up to a hundred essays (!) a day, and it's inevitable that some topics will be repeated. Therefore, the most important thing to do once you've chosen a topic is to stand out in some way. Explore nuances that other students would not. Write with details and clarity that will impress. Have a strong personal voice that can only be your own.

# COMMON ESSAY MISTAKES:

There are many common pitfalls when answering this prompt. We've mentioned them here so you can avoid them as you're brainstorming and writing.

## Ego

This is likely the biggest pitfall for this prompt. Even though this prompt mentions "accomplishment," this does NOT mean to list things from your resume in this essay. Don't mention dollar amounts of fundraisers you've organized, the number of members in the club you started, or the news coverage your protest garnered. *This is not the point of this essay.* Sometimes it can be tempting to mention some of your proudest moments briefly, just to make sure admissions committees are aware. Don't worry, your accomplishments will not go unnoticed. There will be other places on your application to mention championships, grades, and awards. The Common App essay is not the place to mention these things, and readers can spot humble-bragging from a mile away.

One of the things admissions committees hate most is an arrogant student. Avoid boasting aka "humble-bragging" aka ego at all costs. Admissions committees do not want overconfident students on their campus as they tend to be poor team players and think they already know it all. While this prompt does give you the option to mention an accomplishment, try to think of "accomplishment" in terms of personal growth rather than academic or extracurricular achievements. For example, finding a passion for journalism and improving your investigative skills would be the "accomplishment" instead of getting a publication or writing award. Developing strong working relationships with local industry leaders would be the "accomplishment" instead of earning a competitive internship at a company.

## Not Enough Personal Growth

The college experience is often synonymous with exposure to new ideas and subjects. Admissions committee want to recruit diverse thinkers who will not only devour knowledge but also interact with the ideas they are exposed to. Furthermore, they want students who will contribute thoughtfully to discussions in class and apply knowledge in useful ways. This type of personal growth is at the heart of this prompt. There's a lot of value in showing that you've already started doing some of these things by high school. You don't have to make waves in your community or have a 180 degree turn in your goals to show that you're capable of personal growth.

## Overly Complicated Writing

While you want your essay to be creative and show your personality, you don't want to be too quirky. Don't be too sarcastic or humorous or use extended metaphors that leave the reader scratching their head. Definitely don't make up scenarios, because they often come across as inauthentic. Avoid using too many rhetorical questions, em dashes, or lengthy compound-complex sentences. Write to communicate, not to impress.

The Common App essay also has a 650-word limit, which is not a lot of space to communicate a compelling story. Therefore, avoid overly complicating your essay with extended metaphors, long storylines, and unnecessary description. Simple language is better than using jargon. Concrete examples are better than abstract concepts. Specific statements are better than philosophical musings.

## Taking Too Long to Describe the Accomplishment, Event, or Realization

I get it – anything that "sparks a period of personal growth" is probably something that matters to you and something you could write a lot about. However, too many students spend 70% of the essay re-telling the story of what happened rather than the impact of that story. A common example of this mistake occurs with students who write about a trip that sparked personal growth. The students will waste precious essay space describing beautiful mountain landscapes, the poverty of a local African village, or generic observations about how a culture is different from their own. Your essay should be less than 30% telling the story of *what* happened and about 70% breaking down the affect the story had on you.

One way to do this is to limit your storytelling to the introduction and first paragraph(s). Then, you can spend the remainder of the essay diving deeply into insight. The admissions officers aren't trying to see how good of a storyteller you are. Rather, they care about what you took away from an experience. For this prompt, breaking down complex belief systems, personal goals, and potential for change should make up the vast majority of the essay.

## Appearing One-Dimensional

The admissions process at most United States universities is a holistic process. This means that admissions committees are interested in the whole picture of who you are. Not only your grades, awards, test scores, but also how you think, what your goals are, and who you want to become. The Common App essay is a great place to show off surprising and admirable qualities of yourself that your resume would not otherwise show. Therefore, if your major extracurricular activity is a sport, you may not want to write an essay related to sports. If most of your achievements are playing a musical instrument, then don't write an essay about music. If you're mainly a scientist and have conducted research, surprise them by showing your expertise in a different area. Take advantage of the Common App essay to show off unique talents, goals, or life experiences. There will be opportunities to talk about your main academic and extracurricular interests in supplemental essays and interviews.

.

# TOPIC BRAINSTORMING

**Now is the time to write down potential essay ideas. On the next few pages, list anything and everything that you think might be a good essay topic. Don't overthink this part – we're just brainstorming!**

Try to keep in mind the prompt breakdown, topics to avoid, and common mistakes.

## PROMPT

Discuss an accomplishment, event, or realization that sparked a period of personal growth and a new understanding of yourself or others.

1. _____

_____

2. _____

_____

3. _____

_____

4. _____

_____

5. _____

_____

6. _____

_____

7. _____

_____

8. _____

_____

# NARROWING DOWN THE LIST:

**Now, choose three topics to brainstorm more deeply.**

1. _____

    a. Do I have a lot to say about this topic?

    b. What did I learn from this?

    c. How has this experience helped me become a better/more mature person?

**2.** _____

    a. Do I have a lot to say about this topic?

    b. What did I learn from this?

    c. How has this experience helped me become a better/more mature person?

**3.** _____

    a. Do I have a lot to say about this topic?

    b. What did I learn from this?

    c. How has this experience helped me become a better/more mature person?

# Now, choose 1 topic to develop!

## THE CHOSEN TOPIC:

_____

_____

## QUESTIONS TO ANSWER:

Doing this extra work beforehand will be enormously helpful for filling out the essay template later.

- What were your goals or beliefs like *before* the accomplishment, event, or realization?

_____

_____

_____

_____

- Which people in my life impact the way I live and think?

_____

_____

_____

_____

- What was the most important piece of advice I received during high school?

_____

_____

_____

_____

- Do I have a motto I live by? Where did it come from?

_____

_____

_____

_____

- How have my goals changed over time?

  _____

  _____

  _____

  _____

- What are values I live by? Have they always been the same?

  _____

  _____

  _____

  _____

- Which experiences in my life made me question my goals or beliefs?

  _____

  _____

  _____

  _____

- Which extracurricular activities continually challenge me, and in what ways?

_____

_____

_____

_____

- Has this changed your future college/career goals? If so, how?

_____

_____

_____

_____

- What problems do you aim to solve with a club, organization, or business you started or are a member of?

_____

_____

_____

_____

- Who or what do I turn to when I'm unsure of next steps?

  _____

  _____

  _____

  _____

- In what ways am I more mature than a year or two ago?

  _____

  _____

  _____

  _____

- What is my vision for the future? How will I continue to change in the future?

  _____

  _____

  _____

  _____

- How do I know that I have made progress?

_____

_____

_____

_____

# ESSAY OUTLINE

**In the following pages is an easy, brilliant template to help write your essay line-by-line.**

**Here's the outline we'll use:**

1. **Introduction:** we'll establish the setting of what it was like "before" the accomplishment, event, or realization.

2. **Paragraph 1:** we'll describe the accomplishment, event, or realization.

3. **Paragraph 2:** we'll explain the steps you took to improve yourself afterwards.

4. **Paragraph 3:** we'll show your personal growth through specific examples.

5. **Conclusion:** we'll reflect on how your experience will affect your future.

**In the following pages, simply fill in each box in complete sentences. When you finish, you'll have a complete first draft!**

# Ready, Set,

# *Fill In The Essay!*

Remember to answer the question in each box using **complete sentences.**

# Introduction Paragraph

| | |
|---|---|
| Introduction statement related to the topic– a line of dialogue, a quote, a fun fact, or a vivid description. | *Example: Every male in my family, from my great-great-grandfather to my father, has proudly served in the United States military.* |
| Describe the status quo. What was life like before you experienced the accomplishment, event, or | *Example: My family always went over-the-top for Fourth of July celebrations and Memorial Day. My grandfather can name over 100 historical generals and the battles they fought. My brother was recently deployed for a second tour of Afghanistan. They feel a call of duty beyond serving their country – military service runs as deep in my family as blood.* |

| | |
|---|---|
| realization? Give specific examples of this in everyday life. | |
| Tell me what YOU were like before the personal growth. Give me an example of you adhering to old habits or beliefs before this experience. | *Example: As a first-born son, I always assumed I would do the same. I grew up knowing that I wanted to join this family of servicemen, never thinking about other career options. Boy Scout expeditions and shooting ranges occupied my summer breaks.* |

| | |
|---|---|
| | *Example: I was convinced I would answer the call one I turned eighteen. Had it not been for a conversation I had with a young military recruiter, I would be at boot camp instead of applying for an undergraduate education.* |
| Admit that you probably wouldn't have changed unless this event had happened. | |

# Paragraph 1

What were you doing moments before the accomplishment, event, or realization? Briefly explain where you were and why you were there.

WHO or WHAT was involved in the accomplishment, event, or realization?

How was that
day different
than usual?
What prompted
the
accomplishment,
event, or
realization?

What was your
initial reaction or

response to what
happened?

Explain any initial
doubts or
questions you
had about what
happened.

Looking back,
did you know

that you were
about to
undergo a
period of
personal growth?
Why or why not?

# Paragraph 2

Point out the
specific problem
or area of
improvement you
noticed in
yourself, others, or
society after this
event.

Talk about why
you felt the need
to address this
problem or area
of improvement.
Show why you
cared and felt

strongly about this
issue.

Acknowledge
that it was hard to
change your old
habits or beliefs.
Admit that the
issue at hand is
complex, and you
tried to fully
understand the
situation through
research and
conversations with
others.

Explain what the
initial goal you set
for yourself was as
you prepared to
actively improve
on something.

Express
uncertainty or
doubt you felt in
the beginning,
but why it was
important to
make the effort.

# Paragraph 3

Give specific
examples of simple
actions you took in
the weeks and
months after the
accomplishment,
event, or realization.
Show that you were
committed to this
issue over time.

Give a specific
example of working
with or turning to
other people as you

tried to work on
personal growth.

Give a specific
example of failure
when you tried to
encourage personal
growth but faced
difficulty. What was
hard about it?

What was the
immediate impact of
your efforts? How did

your efforts make
something better or
easier for you or
others?

How did you know
that you were
making progress
towards personal
growth or self-
improvement? Did
someone point it
out? Did outcomes
change for the
better?

# Conclusion Paragraph

Summarize the
state of things
today. Is there
anything that still
bothers you? If so,
how do you
continue to try to
make things
better?

What was a time
recently when you
realized you still
had a lot of
personal growth
left to do? Show

how the skills you
learned previously
helped in this
situation.

In the future, how
will you try to
continue to
critically think ways
you can be a
better person?
Why is this type of
continual self-
reflection
important?

What can you do
on a college
campus to seek
others who will
inspire and
challenge you to
become a better
person?

Why is it important
to remember this
experience even
after college?

Why are you a
better or more
well-rounded
person because of
what happened?
How do you
anticipate you'll
continue to grow?

**For your convenience, there are two more blank essay templates in the following pages if you'd like to try writing about other topics.**

# Introduction Paragraph

| | |
|---|---|
| Introduction statement related to the topic– a line of dialogue, a quote, a fun fact, or a vivid description. | *Example: Every male in my family, from my great-great-grandfather to my father, has proudly served in the United States military.* |
| Describe the status quo. What was life like before you experienced the accomplishment, event, or | *Example: My family always went over-the-top for Fourth of July celebrations and Memorial Day. My grandfather can name over 100 historical generals and the battles they fought. My brother was recently deployed for a second tour of Afghanistan. They feel a call of duty beyond serving their country – military service runs as deep in my family as blood.* |

| | |
|---|---|
| realization? Give specific examples of this in everyday life. | |
| Tell me what YOU were like before the personal growth. Give me an example of you adhering to old habits or beliefs before this experience. | *Example: As a first-born son, I always assumed I would do the same. I grew up knowing that I wanted to join this family of servicemen, never thinking about other career options. Boy Scout expeditions and shooting ranges occupied my summer breaks.* |

| | |
|---|---|
| Admit that you probably wouldn't have changed unless this event had happened. | *Example: I was convinced I would answer the call one I turned eighteen. Had it not been for a conversation I had with a young military recruiter, I would be at boot camp instead of applying for an undergraduate education.* |

# Paragraph 1

What were you
doing moments
before the
accomplishment,
event, or
realization?
Briefly explain
where you were
and why you
were there.

WHO or WHAT
was involved in
the
accomplishment,
event, or
realization?

How was that
day different
than usual?
What prompted
the
accomplishment,
event, or
realization?

What was your
initial reaction or

response to what
happened?

Explain any initial
doubts or
questions you
had about what
happened.

Looking back,
did you know

that you were
about to
undergo a
period of
personal growth?
Why or why not?

# Paragraph 2

Point out the
specific problem
or area of
improvement you
noticed in
yourself, others, or
society after this
event.

Talk about why
you felt the need
to address this
problem or area
of improvement.
Show why you
cared and felt

strongly about this issue.

Acknowledge that it was hard to change your old habits or beliefs. Admit that the issue at hand is complex, and you tried to fully understand the situation through research and conversations with others.

Explain what the
initial goal you set
for yourself was as
you prepared to
actively improve
on something.

Express
uncertainty or
doubt you felt in
the beginning,
but why it was
important to
make the effort.

# Paragraph 3

Give specific
examples of simple
actions you took in
the weeks and
months after the
accomplishment,
event, or realization.
Show that you were
committed to this
issue over time.

Give a specific
example of working
with or turning to
other people as you

tried to work on
personal growth.

Give a specific
example of failure
when you tried to
encourage personal
growth but faced
difficulty. What was
hard about it?

What was the
immediate impact of
your efforts? How did

your efforts make
something better or
easier for you or
others?

How did you know
that you were
making progress
towards personal
growth or self-
improvement? Did
someone point it
out? Did outcomes
change for the
better?

# Conclusion Paragraph

Summarize the
state of things
today. Is there
anything that still
bothers you? If so,
how do you
continue to try to
make things
better?

What was a time
recently when you
realized you still
had a lot of
personal growth
left to do? Show

how the skills you
learned previously
helped in this
situation.

In the future, how
will you try to
continue to
critically think ways
you can be a
better person?
Why is this type of
continual self-
reflection
important?

What can you do on a college campus to seek others who will inspire and challenge you to become a better person?

Why is it important to remember this experience even after college?

Why are you a
better or more
well-rounded
person because of
what happened?
How do you
anticipate you'll
continue to grow?

# Introduction Paragraph

| | |
|---|---|
| Introduction statement related to the topic– a line of dialogue, a quote, a fun fact, or a vivid description. | *Example: Every male in my family, from my great-great-grandfather to my father, has proudly served in the United States military.* |
| Describe the status quo. What was life like before you experienced the accomplishment, event, or | *Example: My family always went over-the-top for Fourth of July celebrations and Memorial Day. My grandfather can name over 100 historical generals and the battles they fought. My brother was recently deployed for a second tour of Afghanistan. They feel a call of duty beyond serving their country – military service runs as deep in my family as blood.* |

| | |
|---|---|
| realization? Give specific examples of this in everyday life. | |
| Tell me what YOU were like before the personal growth. Give me an example of you adhering to old habits or beliefs before this experience. | *Example: As a first-born son, I always assumed I would do the same. I grew up knowing that I wanted to join this family of servicemen, never thinking about other career options. Boy Scout expeditions and shooting ranges occupied my summer breaks.* |

| | |
|---|---|
| Admit that you probably wouldn't have changed unless this event had happened. | *Example: I was convinced I would answer the call one I turned eighteen. Had it not been for a conversation I had with a young military recruiter, I would be at boot camp instead of applying for an undergraduate education.* |

# Paragraph 1

What were you
doing moments
before the
accomplishment,
event, or
realization?
Briefly explain
where you were
and why you
were there.

WHO or WHAT
was involved in
the
accomplishment,
event, or
realization?

How was that
day different
than usual?
What prompted
the
accomplishment,
event, or
realization?

What was your
initial reaction or

response to what
happened?

Explain any initial
doubts or
questions you
had about what
happened.

Looking back,
did you know

that you were
about to
undergo a
period of
personal growth?
Why or why not?

# Paragraph 2

Point out the
specific problem
or area of
improvement you
noticed in
yourself, others, or
society after this
event.

Talk about why
you felt the need
to address this
problem or area
of improvement.
Show why you
cared and felt

strongly about this issue.

Acknowledge that it was hard to change your old habits or beliefs. Admit that the issue at hand is complex, and you tried to fully understand the situation through research and conversations with others.

Explain what the
initial goal you set
for yourself was as
you prepared to
actively improve
on something.

Express
uncertainty or
doubt you felt in
the beginning,
but why it was
important to
make the effort.

# Paragraph 3

Give specific
examples of simple
actions you took in
the weeks and
months after the
accomplishment,
event, or realization.
Show that you were
committed to this
issue over time.

Give a specific
example of working
with or turning to
other people as you

tried to work on
personal growth.

Give a specific
example of failure
when you tried to
encourage personal
growth but faced
difficulty. What was
hard about it?

What was the
immediate impact of
your efforts? How did

your efforts make
something better or
easier for you or
others?

How did you know
that you were
making progress
towards personal
growth or self-
improvement? Did
someone point it
out? Did outcomes
change for the
better?

## Conclusion Paragraph

Summarize the
state of things
today. Is there
anything that still
bothers you? If so,
how do you
continue to try to
make things
better?

What was a time
recently when you
realized you still
had a lot of
personal growth
left to do? Show

how the skills you
learned previously
helped in this
situation.

In the future, how
will you try to
continue to
critically think ways
you can be a
better person?
Why is this type of
continual self-
reflection
important?

What can you do
on a college
campus to seek
others who will
inspire and
challenge you to
become a better
person?

Why is it important
to remember this
experience even
after college?

Why are you a
better or more
well-rounded
person because of
what happened?
How do you
anticipate you'll
continue to grow?

# CONGRATULATIONS!

## YOU'VE JUST WRITTEN THE FIRST DRAFT OF YOUR COMMON APP ESSAY!

This is a great accomplishment. The best Common App essays take many drafts, many edits and revisions, and many hours. With the completion of this workbook, you're well on your way to writing a compelling application essay.

Your next steps should be to add your personal voice, writing style, and flair. Get feedback from trusted teachers, parents/mentors, and peers. Make each draft better than the last. Write and Rewrite!

If you'd like to try writing on a different prompt, then check out other Fill In The Essay guides for the Common App essay available on Amazon.

Best of luck!

*-Fill In The Essay Team*
*Fillintheessay.com*
*fillintheessay@gmail.com*

Made in the USA
Middletown, DE
23 April 2023

29365159R00056